GLORY

SCRIPTURES & PRAYERS TO
M A N I F E S T
GOD'S PRESENCE
I N Y O U R L I F E

JOSHUA MILLS

This Book Is Presented To:

_____

By:

_____

Date:

_____

The GLORY

SCRIPTURES & PRAYERS TO
M A N I F E S T
GOD'S PRESENCE
I N   Y O U R   L I F E

JOSHUA MILLS

International Glory Ministries
P.O. Box 4037
Palm Springs, CA 92263
JoshuaMills.com
info@joshuamills.com

Published by New Wine International, Inc
Editing and layout by Harold McDougal
Cover design by Ken Vail

ISBN: 978-1-61917-005-6

Printed in the United States of America

Dedication

This book is dedicated to every person who has a deep longing to live in the glory of God and to my friend, Rev. Jane Lowder, who showed me that it was possible.

Introduction

I've personally discovered that something powerful transpires in our lives when we allow the glory in the Word to become our personal revelation. Revelation ultimately gives birth to manifestation. If you want to experience miracles, you must remain in the presence of God's miracle-working Word. Hear it … believe it … speak it … and see it! You will always prosper in the place where truth is revealed.

If you want to experience healing in your life, you must remain in the presence of God's healing Word. And it's the same for the manifestation of His glory. This can only happen one way: faith comes by hearing the Word of God, and the Spirit wants to give us new faith for His glory.

In this book, I've compiled scriptures, personal prayers and affirmations that will open up this new glory for you as you read them and pray them aloud over your home, family, business, ministry and region. May you experience and stand in the cloud of His goodness as you discover the power of *The GLORY*.

Joshua Mills

> I can experience the Glory fully because
> I know the One who is the Glory!

Who is like to You, O Lord,
among the gods? who is like
You, glorious in holiness, fearful
in praises, doing wonders?
– Exodus 15:11

The GLORY

Father, in the name of Jesus, I exalt You and lift You up. I give You all of my praise and adoration. You are the Glory of my life. You alone are holy. You alone are worthy to be praised. You are the one and only God who works miracles and wonders. There is no one else like You.

> I do not walk in darkness, because
> God's light is with me.

And Moses went up into the mount, and a cloud covered the mount. And the glory of the LORD abode upon mount Sinai, and the cloud covered it six days: and the seventh day he called to Moses out of the midst of the cloud. And the sight of the glory of the LORD was like devouring fire on the top of the mount in the eyes of the children of Israel. And Moses went into the midst of the cloud … .
– Exodus 24:15-18

The GLORY

Father, in the name of Jesus, I seek You and Your glory above all else. Thank You for inviting me into the midst of the cloud, to experience Your light and Your glory more fully. I will not be afraid. I will not fear. I will give myself completely to the work of Your consuming fire, as I pursue the purposes of Your presence. Your light is bringing clarity. Your fire is burning away needless anxieties. Your glory is drawing me up into a realm of becoming everything You have ever purposed for me to be.

~3~

> I have gained wisdom and
> knowledge through the presence
> of God's glory in my life.

*And it came to pass, as Moses entered
into the tabernacle, the cloudy pillar
descended, and stood at the door of the
tabernacle, and the Lord talked with
Moses. And all the people saw the
cloudy pillar stand at the tabernacle
door: and all the people rose up and
worshiped, every man in his tent door.
And the Lord spoke to Moses face to
face, as a man speaks to his friend ... .*
– Exodus 33:9-11

The GLORY

Father, in the name of Jesus, Your glory is welcomed here in my life. May others see you, even as they see me. Let the glory of Your face rest upon my countenance. Let the works of Your hands be the works of my hands. I desire to live, face to face in synchronicity with You.

Let me only speak words that bring edification, encouragement and comfort to those around me. That others might hear You ... see You ... know You ... and feel You through the atmosphere that surrounds my life. Thank You for being my closest Friend.

I have a higher understanding of God's works because I have a higher understanding of His glory.

And he said, I beseech [beg] you, show me Your glory. And he said, I will make all my goodness pass before you, and I will proclaim the name of the LORD before you; and will be gracious to whom I will be gracious, and will show mercy on whom I will show mercy.
— Exodus 33:18-19

The GLORY

Father, in the name of Jesus, I welcome the revelation of Your goodness. Let Your glory pass before me, giving me a vision of You. I know that as I see You, I'll begin to comprehend Your grace and mercy toward me and toward others. May I be transformed by this revelation, to bless the world around me.

I see an opportunity to spread God's glory in every situation that surrounds me.

And the LORD descended in the cloud, and stood with him there, and proclaimed [made known] the name of the LORD. And the LORD passed by before him, and proclaimed, The LORD, The LORD God, merciful and gracious, longsuffering, and abundant in goodness and truth.
– Exodus 34:5-6

The GLORY

Father, in the name of Jesus, I thank You for the cloud of Your glory that covers my life. As You proclaim Yourself as merciful, gracious, longsuffering and abundant in goodness and truth, may I know You fully in this way, as I rest in the proclamation of Your name.

I can see more blessings and favor coming into my life because of God's glory.

Then a cloud covered the tent of the congregation, and the glory of the Lord filled the tabernacle. And Moses was not able to enter into the tent of the congregation, because the cloud abode thereon, and the glory of the Lord filled the tabernacle.
— Exodus 40:34-35

The GLORY

Father, in the name of Jesus, I give You permission to fill my temple (body, soul and spirit) with the outpouring of Your glory. May Your glory fill me completely, until Your manifest presence is the only thing that is evident in my life. I want Your goodness to be seen. I want Your blessing to be seen. I want Your favor to be seen. I want YOU to be seen in me.

I have been given access to God's glory so that His glory can have access through me.

But as truly as I live, all the
earth shall be filled with
the glory of the LORD.
— **Numbers 14:21**

The GLORY

Father, in the name of Jesus, I desire to see the whole earth filled with your glory. Use me to make Your glory known throughout my spheres of influence. I desire to see Your glory touching my home. I desire to see Your glory touching my community. I desire to see Your glory touching all of my business affairs and personal dealings. I know that whatever Your glory touches begins to change. I want to see Your glory touching every area of my life.

I pray for other people to see the glory in the same way that I do.

*And you said, Behold, the L*ORD *our God has showed us His glory and His greatness, and we have heard His voice out of the midst of the fire: we have seen this day that God does talk with man, and He lives.*
– Deuteronomy 5:24

The GLORY

Father, in the name of Jesus, I praise You for the way You've manifested Your glory in the past. Thank You for appearing visibly to the children of Israel on the mountain, in the midst of the fire. I believe that You are the same yesterday, today and forever and that You will tangibly manifest Your glory today for those who are seeking You. Help me to notice Your glory, and let me discern Your voice, so that I can join with the tribes and elders in saying, "I have seen this day that God does talk with man, and He lives!"

I am fulfilled when I follow God's instructions and yield to His glory.

And it came to pass, when the priests were come out of the holy place, that the cloud filled the house of the Lord, so that the priests could not stand to minister because of the cloud: for the glory of the Lord had filled the house of the Lord.
– 1 Kings 8:10-11

The GLORY

Father, in the name of Jesus, I want to live in the atmosphere of Your glory. Nothing satisfies me more than living in Your presence day to day. When I'm in Your glory, I can hear Your voice giving me divine instruction. When I'm in Your glory, I am given bold faith for the task at hand. When I'm in Your glory, I am willing and obedient to do Your bidding. I'm so grateful that You fill my life with the atmosphere of Your glory, so that I can experience You everywhere I go.

I have great confidence in the power of God's glory to lead me, keep me and strengthen me all the days of my life.

Yours, O Lord is the greatness, and the power, and the glory, and the victory, and the majesty … . You are exalted as head above all. Both riches and honor come of You, and You reign over all; and in Your hand is power and might; and in Your hand it is to make great, and to give strength to all.
– 1 Chronicles 29:11-12

The GLORY

Father, in the name of Jesus, I lift up Your name! I give You thanksgiving and praise because You are great. You impart Your greatness and strength to those who recognize and honor You. Teach me to walk in Your power and Your victory, as I allow Your kingdom to be established in my life. I know that true riches and strength can only come from You, because You are exalted over all. Be exalted in my life.

> I am grateful for every blessing that God has given to me from the glory.

Now when Solomon had made an end of praying, the fire came down from heaven, and consumed the burned offering and the sacrifices; and the glory of the LORD filled the house. And the priests could not enter into the house of the LORD, because the glory of the LORD had filled the LORD's house.
– 2 Chronicles 7:1-2

The GLORY

Father, in the name of Jesus, You are good and Your mercy endures forever! I honor You and worship You because You are the God of all glory! I know that every good and perfect thing in my life comes from You. Just like the priests at the dedication of Solomon's temple, I want to humbly bow myself before You. Let Your fire consume the sacrifice! Let Your glory fill my temple! I need the manifestation of Your glory in my life, more than anything else. I live for Your glory. I live for You.

I will not let problems bring me down, I
will stand up and overcome in the glory.

*... Stand up and bless the LORD your
God for ever and ever: and blessed be
Your glorious name, which is exalted
above all blessing and praise.*
– Nehemiah 9:5

The GLORY

Father, in the name of Jesus, You are the glory and the strength of my life! I will stand up and proclaim the greatness of who You are everywhere I go. I live to praise You. I live to worship You. I live to know You in Your glory. Your glorious name is great, and I will sing about it all the days of my life.

I have received the approval of God, so
I don't rely on the approval of others.

O Lord, our Lord, how excellent is
Your name in all the earth! who have
set Your glory above the heavens.
– Psalm 8:1

The GLORY

Father, in the name of Jesus, how excellent is Your name! I can remain in confidence when I come to You because I know that Your name is higher than any other name, and that the power of Your glory overshadows every other thing. Your name is above sickness and disease, and Your glory provides healing. Your name is above poverty and lack, and Your glory supplies for my every need. Your name is above every problem I might face, and Your glory provides abundant miracles. I will rest in the provision of Your glory and in the power of Your name.

The greatness of God's glory
is the strength of my life.

*The heavens declare [are telling of]
the glory of God; and the firmament
[expanse] shows his handywork.*
– Psalm 19:1

The GLORY

Father, in the name of Jesus, when I feel weak, I know that You are strong. When I feel fearful, I know that You are bold. When I feel like giving up, I know that You are faithful. I will choose to stay aligned with You in all things at all times. When I align myself with Your glory, You work all things together for my good, so I can declare the mighty works You have done.

15

I am able to live a rich and satisfying life because the King of Glory resides in me.

Lift up your heads, O you gates; and be you lift up, you everlasting doors; and the King of glory shall come in. Who is this King of glory? The LORD strong and mighty, the LORD mighty in battle. Lift up your heads, O you gates; even lift them up, you everlasting doors; and the King of glory shall come in. Who is this King of glory? The LORD of hosts, He is the King of glory. Selah.
– Psalm 24:7-10

The GLORY

Father, in the name of Jesus, I choose to make room for Your glory. Right now, I am opening up the doorways of my spirit, soul and body, so that You can have complete access to every part of my life. I want You to be the King of Glory resident inside of me. I give You permission to rule and reign with Your strength, mercy and might. Help me to recognize Your kingly authority, so that I can fully live in Your kingdom realities.

16

I can trust the voice of glory because
it is for me, not against me.

*The voice of the LORD is upon the
waters: the God of glory thunders:
the LORD is upon many waters. The
voice of the LORD is powerful; the
voice of the LORD is full of majesty.*
– Psalm 29:3-4

The GLORY

Father, in the name of Jesus, when You speak I will listen. I will pay attention to every word that comes from Your lips. I know that Your powerful words come to bring me into complete freedom and truth. I will listen to hear the thunder of Your majestic voice, but I will also discern Your still small voice that speaks gently to my heart with kindness. I don't want to miss a single word, but I want to live my life in perfect obedience to Your voice.

17

I am a complete person because I
live in the fullness of glory.

Be You exalted, O God, above
the heavens; let Your glory
be above all the earth.
– Psalm 57:5

The GLORY

Father, in the name of Jesus, I've discovered my wholeness in You. Because of Your life, I can now live fully. In You, I live and breathe and find my true identity. Thank You for introducing me to my true self, as You've introduced me to Your glory. I choose to live in Your glory fully, without any hindrances. Your glory has set me above my problems and positioned me for divine success. Be exalted in my life.

18

I see the beauty in others, when
I see with the eyes of glory.

To see Your power and Your glory, so
as I have seen You in the sanctuary.
– Psalm 63:2

The GLORY

Father, in the name of Jesus, thank You for giving me God-vision. The more I see You in Your glory, the more I see the world around me through the eyes of Your Spirit. Thank You for changing my perspective, so that I can walk in Your love, peace, mercy, grace and power everywhere I go.

19

I live in divine peace, because my
world is filled with God's glory.

*And blessed be His glorious name for
ever: and let the whole earth be filled
with his glory; Amen, and Amen.*
— Psalm 72:19

The GLORY

Father, in the name of Jesus, I am so glad that I don't need to live in anxiety or fear because Your glory surrounds me on a daily basis. I will not be afraid of problems that come my way. I will not become discouraged by what others do or say because my whole world is filled with Your glory and Your light. Blessed be Your glorious name! My whole world is filled with Your glory.

20

I am filled with good things because
I choose to walk in the glory.

For the LORD God is a sun and shield:
the LORD will give grace and glory:
no good thing will he withhold
from them that walk uprightly.
– Psalm 84:11

The GLORY

Father, in the name of Jesus, I delight in Your good and perfect gifts. Because You are my Sun and Shield, I am comforted, knowing that You deflect every evil assignment that's been set against me. I can live securely in Your glory, knowing that as I live for You, I will have Your grace and glory for any situation that comes my way.

21

I am being changed by God's glory,
so that only God can be seen in me.

When the LORD shall build up Zion,
He shall appear in His glory.
— Psalm 102:16

The GLORY

Father, in the name of Jesus, let the revelation of Your glory consume my life completely. As I am built up in faith, anointing and glory, I can sense a greater awareness of Your divine presence. Let this manifestation flow on me, over me and through me. Your glory is appearing more and more, as You change me by Your glory day by day.

22

I am aware of God's supernatural
abilities and it's becoming my reality.

*Bless the LORD, O my soul. O LORD
my God, You are very great; You are
clothed with honor and majesty. Who
covers Yourself with light as with
a garment: who stretches out the
heavens like a curtain: who lays the
beams of His chambers in the waters:
who makes the clouds His chariot:
who walks upon the wings of the wind.*
– Psalm 104:1-3

The GLORY

Father, in the name of Jesus, I recognize Your greatness. You are forever clothed with honor and majesty. Even as You clothe Yourself with light, wrap me in the brilliance of Your garments. I want to shine with Your glory. I want to reflect Your light to the world around me. As you make clouds your chariots and walk upon the wind, teach me how to soar in Your glory with Your spirit light.

23

I am the workmanship of God, and I was created to make a difference.

The glory of the LORD shall endure for ever: the LORD shall rejoice in His works.
– Psalm 104:31

The GLORY

Father, in the name of Jesus, I am so blessed to know that You take great delight in me. Thank You for encouraging me by Your Word, empowering me by Your Spirit and filling my life with Your glory. You make the difference in me. I will let the atmosphere of Your eternal glory change those things which are temporal around me, to bring forth a divine shift everywhere I go.

24

I am the righteousness of God in Christ Jesus, created to show forth His glory!

His work is honorable and glorious:
and His righteousness endures for ever.
– Psalm 111:3

The GLORY

Father, in the name of Jesus, You are the light of my life. Your glory fills me with bright illumination, to shine in the darkness. I am not afraid of the dark because I know that through You, I am able to radiate Your glory light. Send me to the people, places and atmospheres that need You most. I will shine for You.

25

I am a channel through which God
can bless all nations with His glory.

The LORD is high above all nations,
and His glory above the heavens.
– Psalm 113:4

The GLORY

Father, in the name of Jesus, I ask for the nations. I want to see Your glorious Gospel of light, love and grace flood every tribe, every tongue and every nation with Your saving power. As I come into contact with others, anoint my lips to speak Your blessings. Anoint my hands with Your healing touch. Anoint my actions to display Your kindness. Anoint my heart with Your love for those who are lost. Use me to bless all nations with Your glory.

26

I can release songs of glory because
God's glory song resides in me.

Yea, they shall sing in the ways of the
Lord: for great is the glory of the Lord.
– Psalm 138:5

The GLORY

Father, in the name of Jesus, You are the song that I sing! Thank You for giving me a new song of worship each and every day. As I consider You and Your ways, I always find a reason to praise.

I am a voice for God's glory, to be heard, understood and received.

I will speak of the glorious honor of Your majesty, and of Your wondrous works.
— Psalm 145:5

The GLORY

Father, in the name of Jesus, I trust Your voice. I know that You mean what You say. You always watch over Your Word to perform it. Let Your words be in my mouth, so that I can speak with the authority of Heaven. I will declare your honor, majesty and wonderful works, and as I do, I know that You will bring the manifestation of that revelation.

28

I will speak of God's Kingdom power because I am a son/daughter of God's glorious Kingdom.

All Your works shall praise You, O LORD; and Your saints shall bless You. They shall speak of the glory of Your kingdom, and talk of Your power; to make known to the sons of men His mighty acts, and the glorious majesty of His kingdom.
– Psalm 145:10-12

The GLORY

Father, in the name of Jesus, what a privilege it is to live for You! I am blessed to be a child in Your Kingdom. I am blessed to live in the realm of Your mighty power and glory! Thank You for displaying Your miracles, signs and wonders around my life, even as I speak about Your goodness. I want the whole world to know how glorious You are.

29

I am secure and protected within the glory.

And the LORD will create upon every dwelling place of mount Zion, and upon her assemblies, a cloud and smoke by day, and the shining of a flaming fire by night: for upon all the glory shall be a defense.
– Isaiah 4:5

The GLORY

Father, in the name of Jesus, I know that I can rest safely in Your glory. Surround me today within the billows of Your smoky presence. Hide me securely within the cloud of Your weighty glory. At night, be the flaming fire that defends me in the midst of the darkness. I will not fear any evil, because I trust in You. I trust in Your glory.

30

> I am the temple for God's Spirit,
> and His glory resides in me.

*I saw also the L*ORD *sitting upon a
throne, high and lifted up, and His train
[trailing edge of His robe] filled the
temple. Above it stood the seraphims:
each one had six wings; with two
he covered his face, and with two he
covered his feet, and with two he did
fly. And one cried to another, and said,
Holy, holy, holy, is the L*ORD *of hosts:
the whole earth is full of His glory.*
– Isaiah 6:1-3

The GLORY

Father, in the name of Jesus, I invite all of You
to fill all of me. I offer You my spirit, soul and body,
as a temple for Your glory. May You be high and
lifted up within me. Let Your angels surround me on
every side. I want to live my life today so that none
of me can be seen, but only all of You, in all of Your
glory. Let Your glory be magnified in my life.

31

I find my joy in the glory of God.

The wilderness and the solitary place shall be glad for them; and the desert shall rejoice, and blossom as the rose. It shall blossom abundantly, and rejoice even with joy and singing: the glory of Lebanon shall be given to it, the excellency of Carmel and Sharon, they shall see the glory of the LORD, and the excellency of our God.
– Isaiah 35:1-2

The GLORY

Father, in the name of Jesus, Your joy is the overcoming strength of my life. In the wilderness seasons, when I feel weary, I have Your promise that You will never forsake me. Even in the times that seem as desolate as a desert, You give me a reason to rejoice. Your Word brings me life, Your anointing comes to deliver, and Your glory causes joy to arise within me. In Your manifest presence I find my joy.

I will rise and shine in the brilliance of the glory. Nothing can diminish my light.

Arise, shine; for your light is come, and the glory of the LORD is risen upon you. For, behold, the darkness shall cover the earth, and gross darkness the people: but the LORD shall arise upon you, and His glory shall be seen upon you. And the Gentiles [nations] shall come to your light, and kings to the brightness of your rising.
– Isaiah 60:1-3

The GLORY

Father, in the name of Jesus, Your light shines brighter than the noonday sun! I can feel Your light arising within me. Every area of darkness in my life is being overtaken by the powerful rays of Your brilliant light. Your glory light overcomes sickness. Your glory light overcomes despair. Your glory light overcomes grief. Your glory light overcomes every enemy assignment that attempts to harm me. As Your light shines within me, Your glory is seen upon me. Let there be light!

33

I can walk in the light of God's
glory everywhere I go.

The sun shall be no more your light
by day; neither for brightness shall
the moon give light to you: but the
Lord shall be to you an everlasting
light, and your God your glory.
– Isaiah 60:19

The GLORY

Father, in the name of Jesus, You are my ever-lasting light! You are my glory and the radiance of Heaven that leads the way. I will follow Your light because I choose to follow You. As You open up new spiritual pathways for me to walk in, I know that I am being led into my divine inheritance. I will walk in Your light as You are glorified in my life.

34

I am a display of God's splendor
for the entire world to behold.

You shall also be a crown of
glory in the hand of the LORD,
and a royal diadem [i.e. turban]
in the hand of your God.
– Isaiah 62:3

The GLORY

Father, in the name of Jesus, I am Your treasure. I will be careful to guard this precious gift that You've given to me. I will not live carelessly or recklessly, but I choose to honor You in word and deed. Help me to guard myself against those who would try to harm me and those who would want to steal the precious things of the Spirit from my life. Give me wise discernment, a heart of wisdom and eyes for Your glory. I want to live my life so that those around me can always see Your glory in me.

35

> I am willing to surrender my own will so that God's will can be perfected in my life.

As the appearance of the bow that is in the cloud in the day of rain, so was the appearance of the brightness round about. This was the appearance of the likeness of the glory of the LORD. And when I saw it, I fell upon my face, and I heard a voice of one that spoke.
– Ezekiel 1:28

The GLORY

Father, in the name of Jesus, not my will but Yours be done. As I behold the revelation of Your glory, I fall on my face in complete surrender. I bow down to You, for You alone are holy. Speak to me in Your glory, that I may comprehend Your perfect will for my life.

36

I can see clearly because God's
glory gives me vision.

*And, behold, the glory of the God
of Israel was there, according to
the vision that I saw in the plain.*
– Ezekiel 8:4

The GLORY

Father, in the name of Jesus. I ask for a seer's anointing that will anoint my heart with supernatural optics. I want to perceive the ways and wonders of Heaven. I also ask that You would anoint my eyes with prophetic perception to see visions of You in Your glory. May every faculty of my spirit, soul and body be given to Your glory, for Your glory.

37

I receive every promise from God,
when I surrender to His glory.

*And the glory of the God of Israel was
gone up from the cherub, whereupon
he was, to the threshold of the house.
And he called to the man clothed
with linen, which had the writer's
inkhorn [inkstand] by his side.*
– Ezekiel 9:3

The GLORY

Father, in the name of Jesus, thank You for the inkstand of glory that You have provided, so that Your angel of the Lord can write a word of promise upon the foreheads of Your true believers. We long to receive the seal of Your Holy Spirit of promise. Even as our hearts are turned toward Your glory, may Your glory fill every part of our lives.

38

> In the glory, I am surrounded by the presence of God's angels.

And the cherubims lifted up their wings, and mounted up from the earth in my sight: when they went out, the wheels also were beside them, and every one stood at the door of the east gate of the LORD's house; and the glory of the God of Israel was over them above.
– Ezekiel 10:19

The GLORY

Father, in the name of Jesus, I am continually amazed by the awesome presence of Your glory. Thank You for opening my eyes to see spiritual realities and for opening my spirit to receive them fully. I want to learn how to cooperate with Your glory and work with the angels that surround my life.

39

God's glory lifts me into His divine purposes.

Afterward he brought me to the gate, even the gate that looks toward the east: and, behold, the glory of the God of Israel came from the way of the east: and His voice was like a noise of many waters: and the earth shined with His glory … .
So the spirit took me up, and brought me into the inner court; and, behold, the glory of the LORD filled the house.
– Ezekiel 43:1-2 and 5

G_{LORY}

The

Father, in the name of Jesus, I invite You to lift me into every vision that concerns me. I know that without a vision people begin to perish. I want to see what You are revealing in Your glory so that I can prosper in my calling. Give me a willing spirit to receive, and give me eyes to see.

~40~

> I am the earth, and I am being filled
> with the knowledge of God's glory.

For the earth shall be filled with
the knowledge of the glory of the
LORD, *as the waters cover the sea.*
— **Habakkuk 2:14**

The GLORY

Father, in the name of Jesus, thank You for filling me with the knowledge of Your glory. I am fertile soil in which You can sow Your seeds of revelation. I am a generous receiver, and I am making room for Your glory in my life.

41

God's glory presents me with new beginnings.

God came from Teman [like a rising sun from the east], and the Holy One from mount Paran [signaling a new day]. Selah. His glory covered the heavens, and the earth was full of his praise. And his brightness was as the light; he had horns [flashing rays of light] coming out of his hand: and there was the hiding of his power.
– Habakkuk 3:3-4

THE GLORY

Father, in the name of Jesus, I declare that You have broken all darkness over my life. Just like the rising sun, You have initiated a new day for me, dawning with liberating freedom and hope. The radiant splendor of Your light protects me and fills me with Your power for breakthrough! Thank You for covering my life with Your glory. I will sing a new song of praise to You.

42

> In the glory, my latter years will be greater than my former years.

The glory of this latter house shall be greater than of the former, says the Lord of hosts: and in this place will I give peace, says the Lord of hosts.
– Haggai 2:9

The GLORY

Father, in the name of Jesus, I trust every promise in Your Word. I receive an impartation from Your glory today that brings supernatural strength, divine energy, spiritual revitalization and peace that passes all natural understanding. I declare that "the glory of my latter house, is greater than the glory of my former house." You are bringing me into every place of promise.

43

I am empowered with the
strength of God's glory.

For I, says the LORD, will be unto her
a wall of fire round about, and will
be the glory in the midst of her.
– Zechariah 2:5

The GLORY

Father, in the name of Jesus, Your strength is my defense. Thank You for surrounding my life like a blazing barrier of protection. I can sense Your "Messengers of Fire" standing round about me. Your angel armies are fighting my battles, so that I can rest in all of Your glory goodness. Even right now, I can feel Your glory filling my life.

44

I can see the glory because
my heart is pure.

Blessed are the pure in heart:

for they shall see God.
– Matthew 5:8

The GLORY

Father, in the name of Jesus, give me Your eyes to see. I don't want to see life through the eyes of the natural, but I want to see every situation that I encounter through the eyes of the Spirit. I want to see You in everyone and in everything. Give me eyes to see Your glory.

45

> God's glory rescues me from temptation
> and delivers me from all harm.

And lead us not into temptation,
but deliver us from evil: for Yours
is the kingdom, and the power,
and the glory, for ever. Amen.
– Matthew 6:13

The GLORY

Father, in the name of Jesus, I receive Your supernatural deliverance that sets me free from all evil. Because of Your finished work that was sealed through agreement with the blood of Christ, You have delivered me from sickness, poverty, shame, depression, guilt, sin and death. I receive the resurrection life of Your Kingdom, Your power and Your glory right now. Let it ever increase in growing manifestation as I seek to give You glory in spirit, soul and body.

46

The light of God's glory gives me
supernatural understanding.

*While he yet spoke, behold, a bright
cloud overshadowed them: and behold
a voice out of the cloud, which said,
This is my beloved Son, in whom I
am well pleased; hear you Him.*
— **Matthew 17:5**

The GLORY

Father, in the name of Jesus, I invite the bright cloud of Your glory to overshadow my life. I will wait, watch, and listen for Your glory. As You speak to me with clarity and precision, I will be motivated forward by Your holy revelation. My spirit, eyes and ears are open to receive, see and hear You.

47

I am a sign and wonder of
God's glory in the earth.

*And then shall appear the sign of
the Son of man in heaven: and then
shall all the tribes of the earth
mourn, and they shall see the Son of
man coming in the clouds of heaven
with power and great glory.*
– Matthew 24:30

The GLORY

Father, in the name of Jesus, let the signs of Your glory increase in my life, to draw many to the saving knowledge of who You are. I want to be Your supernatural sign on earth, even before the coming of the sign of the Son of Man in Heaven. Make me to shine with Your presence, and may my heart be ready to receive You fully when You come with Your power and great glory.

48

> The overshadowing cloud of
> God's glory gives me clarity.

And there was a cloud that
overshadowed them: and a voice
came out of the cloud, saying, This
is my beloved Son: hear Him.
– Mark 9:7

The GLORY

Father, in the name of Jesus, I desire to be enveloped by Your cloud of glory. Overshadow me in the depths of Your divine wisdom and counsel. My spirit is open to hear You speak to me. I will listen to Your words and simply obey the instructions of Your voice.

49

Fear cannot hold me back. I will
approach God's glory in faith.

*And, lo, the angel [messenger] of the
Lord came upon them, and the glory
of the Lord shone round about them:
and they were sore [very] afraid.*
– Luke 2:9

The GLORY

Father, in the name of Jesus, help me to not be afraid of Your glory presence. I want to stand in Your glory and receive everything You have for me within these realms. I welcome the appearance and interaction of Your heavenly angels. I welcome Your brilliant shining and radiant Shekinah glory. Let Your manifest presence increase more and more in my life.

God's glory changes my entire being.

*While he thus spoke, there came
a cloud, and overshadowed them:
and they feared [were afraid] as
they entered into the cloud.*
– Luke 9:34

The GLORY

Father, in the name of Jesus, I will enter, unafraid, into the cloud of Your glory presence. I will not allow any distractions, past experiences, disappointments or preconceived ideas to hinder me. I open myself fully to You, even as You open Yourself fully to me. I breathe in. I enter into Your cloud of glory and invite You to fill me with the life-changing smoke of Your presence. Even as I go deeper still, I can sense Your glory filling me. I can sense Your glory changing me.

51

I will stand in the glory cloud
and declare God's power!

And then shall they see the
Son of man coming in a cloud
with power and great glory.
– Luke 21:27

The GLORY

Father, in the name of Jesus, as I worship You in Spirit and in truth, I know that something begins to change in the atmosphere. I can feel myself being enveloped by the very cloud of Your presence, and, from within the cloud, I can feel Your power. Thank You for releasing Your power into my life every time I choose to praise and worship You.

52

God's Word brings glory because there is a special glory on the Word.

And the Word was made flesh, and dwelt among us, [and we beheld His glory, the glory as of the only begotten of the Father,] full of grace and truth.
– John 1:14

The GLORY

Father, in the name of Jesus, help me to fully receive the glory on Your Word. I want to walk into new territories of the divine supernatural, and I know that these pathways are opened to me, as I search out Your Word and discover Your glory in it. You are the glory that I seek.

Because I believe in God, I
can see the glory of God.

Jesus says to her, Said I not to
you, that, if you would believe,
you should see the glory of God?
– John 11:40

The GLORY

Father, in the name of Jesus, help me to believe. According to Your Word, I know that I will see the result of my faith in manifestation. Help me to believe in Your Word. Help me to believe in Your promises. Help me to see beyond the temporal circumstances of my current situations. I want to see Your glory.

54

I am in unity with Christ, therefore
I can behold His glory!

Father, I will that they also,
whom You have given Me, be with
Me where I am; that they may
behold My glory, which You have
given Me: for You loved Me before
the foundation of the world.
– John 17:24

The GLORY

Father, in the name of Jesus, thank You for drawing me to Yourself. I surrender my own self-will and selfish desires, so that I might be fully wrapped within Your divine presence. I want to be with You where You are. As I am surrounded by You, I am surrounded to behold Your glory.

55

I am open to see, hear and receive
from the glory of God.

And he said, Men, brethren,
and fathers, hearken [listen];
The God of glory appeared to
our father Abraham … .
– Acts 7:2

The GLORY

Father, in the name of Jesus, I am so thankful that You desire to show me Your glory. Thank You for being so faithful to me and to my spiritual parents who have led the way before me. Thank You for making Yourself known by appearing to Abraham. In the same way that You have shown Yourself to others in the past, I have complete confidence that You will let me see Your glory in this day. God of Glory, I invite You to manifest in my life and my present situations today.

56

I am living under an open heaven. The blessings of God's glory are available to me.

But he, being full of the Holy Ghost, looked up steadfastly [intently] into heaven, and saw the glory of God, and Jesus standing on the right hand of God, and said, Behold, I see the heavens opened, and the Son of man standing on the right hand of God.
— Acts 7:55-56

The GLORY

Father, in the name of Jesus, thank You for filling me with Your Spirit. This Spirit-filled life allows me to look into the heavens with spiritual perception, to see the authority of Christ and all the blessings that You've made available to my life. Thank You for opening Your heavens over me, so that I can live within the glory realm.

57

In the glory, I am united
together with Christ.

And if children, then heirs; heirs of
God, and joint-heirs with Christ; if
so be that we suffer with Him, that
we may be also glorified together.

– Romans 8:17

The GLORY

Father, in the name of Jesus, I praise You for Your faithfulness. As Your child, I am a joint-heir with Christ, to receive the same blessings, victories and breakthroughs in spirit, soul and body. Thank You for raising us up together into all of Your glory goodness.

58

I can live, breathe and move in
the glory realms of God.

Whether therefore you eat, or
drink, or whatsoever you do,
do all to the glory of God.
– 1 Corinthians 10:31

The GLORY

Father, in the name of Jesus, there is no other place that I desire to live, except in the realms of Your glory. I want to live, breathe, eat, drink and move in Your glory realms all the days of my life. Thank You for inviting me into Your divine pattern for heavenly living and teaching me how to move in the Spirit more fully, so that everything I do will be for Your glory.

59

I am going from one level
of glory to the next.

*For if the ministration [ministry] of
condemnation be glory, much more
does the ministration [ministry] of
righteousness exceed in glory. For
even that which was made glorious
had no glory in this respect, by
reason of the glory that excels.*
– 2 Corinthians 3:9-10

The GLORY

Father, in the name of Jesus, I can see in the Spirit that You have so much more available to me than I've experienced to this point. Help me to stay focused and consistent in my pursuit of Your divine presence. I don't want to be satisfied with yesterday's manna, but I want to continually experience the freshness of Your daily bread. Thank You for supernaturally moving me from glory to glory, as You connect me with the people, places and atmospheres that will cause me to grow in the Spirit.

60

In the glory, I am introduced to myself.

*But we all, with open face beholding
as in a glass [mirror] the glory
of the Lord, are changed into the
same image from glory to glory,
even as by the Spirit of the Lord.*
– 2 Corinthians 3:18

The GLORY

Father, in the name of Jesus, Your glory expands my understanding. Increase Your glory around me, upon me and within me, that I might comprehend every divine plan You've purposed for my life. Even as I look into the mirror of Your glory, help me recognize the image of Christ reflected through me, so that I realize that in the glory I can be everything You've dreamed I could be.

61

When I see the face of Jesus,
I see God's glory.

*For God, who commanded the
light to shine out of darkness, has
shined in our hearts, to give the
light of the knowledge of the glory
of God in the face of Jesus Christ.*
– 2 Corinthians 4:6

The GLORY

Father, in the name of Jesus, I want to behold the beautiful face of Your glory. I want to see the many sides of my Savior's face. Give me a beautiful vision of the Lamb of God, and allow me courage to stand in the roar of the Lion of Judah. I want to see into the eyes of the prophetic Eagle-face, and be as lowly as the humble Ox. I want to see the faces of Christ, so that Your light will illuminate within me the many aspects of Your glory.

62

In everything and at all times, I can
see the glory working for me.

For all things are for your sakes, that
the abundant grace might through
the thanksgiving of many redound
[overflow] to the glory of God.
– 2 Corinthians 4:15

The GLORY

Father, in the name of Jesus, help me to recognize the workings of Your glory in the midst of every situation. Even in the most difficult circumstances, I want to see You! I know that You are turning things around for me, working all things together for my benefit. Help me to perceive Your goodness at all times.

63

I am seated in the glory realm.

And God raised us up with Christ
and seated us with him in the
heavenly realms in Christ Jesus.
– Ephesians 2:6 (NIV)

The GLORY

Father, in the name of Jesus, thank You for making room in Your glory for me. I will make room for Your glory in my life. I will choose to remain seated in the blessings of Your glory, in every situation and at all times. Thank You for giving me the privilege of being seated in the heavenly realms, where I find complete peace, rest and ease.

64

I am strong, and my spirit is strengthened in God's glory.

That He would grant you, according
to the riches of His glory, to
be strengthened with might by
His Spirit in the inner man.
– Ephesians 3:16

The GLORY

Father, in the name of Jesus, I know that You are strengthening my spirit-man so that I can rise above every natural difficulty. Thank You for giving me Your strength and power to overcome the troubles of this world. I will walk in Your victorious might, because I am strong in You.

65

I will flow with the move of God's glory today and forever.

To Him be glory in the church by
Christ Jesus throughout all ages,
world without end. Amen.
– Ephesians 3:21

The GLORY

Father, in the name of Jesus, thank You for always keeping me on the cutting edge of Your Spirit. I want to be a pioneer for You. Like a river, I want to continually flow with the movement of Your glory, so that Your global Church will be filled with the knowledge of You and that it might spill out and splash over unto the nations of the earth. Use me as a forerunner in Your glory.

66

I acknowledge God's Lordship over my life, and this brings Him glory.

That at the name of Jesus every knee should bow, of things in heaven, and things in earth, and things under the earth; and that every tongue should confess that Jesus Christ is Lord, to the glory of God the Father.
– Philippians 2:10-11

The GLORY

Father, in the name of Jesus, You are my Lord. I only want to do that which brings You glory. I will live my life bowed before You, and my tongue will always confess that You are Lord over my life. I can do nothing apart from You. No one else compares to You! I will always give You all the glory, honor and praise.

67

I am prosperous. God's glory
abundance is available to me.

*But my God shall supply all
your need according to His riches
in glory by Christ Jesus. Now
to God and our Father be glory
for ever and ever. Amen.*
– Philippians 4:19-20

The GLORY

Father, in the name of Jesus, You have opened up the glorious treasuries of Your abundance to me. I know that in Your glory there is absolutely no lack or insufficiency. Thank You for surrounding me with a whirlwind of divine wealth, so that all I need to do is reach out and receive it. Teach me how to be a generous receiver, so that I can live in this glory forever.

68

I am filled to overflowing with everything I need, because the hope of glory lives in me.

To whom God would make known what is the riches of the glory of this mystery among the Gentiles; which is Christ in you, the hope of glory.

– Colossians 1:27

The GLORY

Father, in the name of Jesus, Your divine revelation changes everything. Thank You for opening the mystery and giving me a vision of who You are inside of me. Your glory has made the way for me to live a rich and satisfying life.

69

In the glory, God sees me for who I am.

When Christ, who is our life,
shall appear, then shall you also
appear with Him in glory.
– Colossians 3:4

The GLORY

Father, in the name of Jesus, Your kindness always leads me to repentance. I am so glad that You don't miss anything, but You see it all. You know my strengths, and You know my weaknesses. Still, through it all, You are kind. Thank You for loving me and always guiding me toward repentance, so that I can live free, healthy and joyful within the realms of Your glory.

70

I am responsible for walking
in the glory, as God calls me to
live in His Kingdom realm.

*That you would walk worthy
of God, who has called you to
His kingdom and glory.*
– 1 Thessalonians 2:12

The GLORY

Father, in the name of Jesus, give me courage to take bold steps today. I want to walk on the water with You. As I walk by greater faith, I know that it will cause me to live in greater glory. Give me the strength, boldness and determination to walk fully into Your supernatural plans for my life.

71

> I can rest in God's glory, because
> Jesus Christ sits on the right
> hand of the Majesty on high.

Who being the brightness of His glory,
and the express image of His person,
and upholding all things by the word
of His power, when He had by Himself
purged our sins, sat down on the
right hand of the Majesty on high.
— Hebrews 1:3

152

The GLORY

Father, in the name of Jesus, I am so glad that You're teaching me how to rest in Your glory. I will fully enter into the ease of this realm. I have complete confidence that all things are upheld by the word of Your power in the brightness of Your glory. I will rest in you and allow Your blessing to be settled in me.

72

Christ's sacrifice has opened the way for
me to experience all of God's glory.

*But we see Jesus, who was made a
little lower than the angels for the
suffering of death, crowned with glory
and honor; that He by the grace of God
should taste death for every man.*
— Hebrews 2:9

The GLORY

Father, in the name of Jesus, I receive all that You've made available to me in the open heavens. I know that an open heaven demands an open earth, so I open myself wide to receive in this atmosphere of Your glory.

73

My understanding is enlarged and I am enlightened by God's excellent glory.

For He received from God the Father honor and glory, when there came such a voice to Him from the excellent glory, This is My beloved Son, in whom I am well pleased.
– 2 Peter 1:17

The GLORY

Father, in the name of Jesus, thank You for expanding my mind in Your glory realm. I will allow Your thoughts to become my thoughts, so that Your ways might also become my ways. Thank You for taking pleasure in me, as I delight in You.

74

I am free to worship God; His glory
gives me a new song to sing.

And after these things I heard
a great voice of many people
in heaven, saying, Alleluia;
Salvation, and glory, and honor,
and power, to the Lord our God.
– Revelation 19:1

The GLORY

Father, in the name of Jesus, the frequency of Your glory is bringing me back into perfect harmony with Your divine will. I can sense the atmosphere changing, as I begin to praise You. I choose to sing with the heavenly choir and declare "Hallelujah, Salvation, and glory, and honor, and power, to the Lord our God."

75

> I can see all the glories of Heaven, because Heaven is open to me.

And I saw heaven opened, and behold a white horse; and He that sat upon him was called Faithful and True, and in righteousness He does judge and make war.
— **Revelation 19:11**

The GLORY

Father, in the name of Jesus, thank You for inviting me into Your glory realm, where I can see things that prepare me for Your greater service. Thank You for filling my mind with the colors, light, and vision of the open heaven, so that I might glimpse a vision of You and Your will.

76

I am illuminated by God's light; His glory shines brightly through me.

And the city had no need of the sun, neither of the moon, to shine in it: for the glory of God did lighten [illuminate] it, and the Lamb [the Lord Jesus Christ] is the light thereof.
– Revelation 21:23

The GLORY

Father, in the name of Jesus, thank You for being the central Light of my life. Let Your glory presence shine through me, to illuminate the darkest places and to flood the most desperate situations with the light of Christ. Let Your healing shine through me. Let Your restorative power shine through me. Let Your peace shine through me. Let Your love shine through me.

77

I love God's glory, and the glory loves me

For God so loved the world, that He gave His only begotten Son, that whoever believes in Him should not perish, but have everlasting life.

– John 3:16

The GLORY

A Prayer of Salvation

Jesus, Thank You for coming into my heart. I invite You to be my Lord and Savior. I give You my sin in exchange for the life that only You can give. Thank You for cleansing me with Your blood and giving me a brand new start. I receive this gift of salvation, and I ask You to fill me with Your glory.

About the Author

Joshua Mills is an internationally recognized ordained minister of the Gospel, as well as a recording artist, keynote conference speaker and author of more than twenty books and spiritual training manuals. He is well known for his unique insights into the glory realm, prophetic sound and the supernatural atmosphere that he carries. Wherever Joshua ministers, the Word of God is confirmed by miraculous signs and wonders that testify of Jesus Christ. For more than twenty years, he has helped people discover the life-shifting truths of living in the Spirit.

Joshua and his wife Janet co-founded International Glory Ministries and have ministered on six continents in over seventy-five nations around the world. Featured in several film documentaries, they have ministered to millions around the world through radio, television and online webcasts.

Joshua Mills has both the first-hand experience and proven revelatory knowledge to teach about the glory and impart that revelation to others.

To contact the author about speaking
invitations, other resources,
upcoming spiritual training seminars
or for prayer, please contact:

International Glory Ministries
P.O. Box 4037
Palm Springs, CA 92263
www.JoshuaMills.com
info@joshuamills.com

Available CDs & Digital
*Downloads by Joshua Mill*s

Declaring His Glory
Heavenly Things: Throne
Room Encounters
Receive Your Healing
Reversing the Clock
SpiritSpa: Piano Instrumental
SpiritSpa 2
Simple Supernatural
The Power of Praise
The Power of the Glory Cloud
The Power of Your Testimony

Physical copies available for order from:

JoshuaMills.com

All albums are also available
for digital download

INTERNATIONAL GLORY

Become a Monthly Partner with International Glory and the miracle ministry of Joshua Mills today! More information available online:

www.JoshuaMills.com

Notes

Notes